Carl Maria von WEBER

CONCERTINO FOR CLARINET

Edited by Charles Neidich

Piano

LAUREN KEISER
MUSIC PUBLISHING

Weber Concertino, Introduction

It was a wonderful accident of fate which brought the young composer Carl Maria von Weber together in 1811 with the great clarinet virtuoso Heinrich Baermann. Weber met Baermann in the town of Darmstadt sometime early in 1811 and having been engaged for a concert in Munich, Baermann's hometown, he asked if Baermann would like to collaborate. Baermann, at that time the more famous of the two, agreed on condition that Weber compose a work for him to play. Weber complied with the Concertino which he finished in three days on April 3rd. Baermann performed the work on April 5 and just two days after, on April 7th the King of Bavaria, who was very impressed both with the work itself and with Baermann's virtuosic rendition, commissioned Weber to write 2 concertos. These Weber soon competed and Baermann premiered both in the same year, the first on June 13 and the second on November 25. Weber went on to write two more works for Baermann, the Variations, op. 33 and the Quintet op. 48. The Gran Duo Concertante, composed most likely for Baermann's colleague and rival, Johann Hermstedt completed Weber's oeuvre for clarinet, a body of work which along with that of Mozart, Spohr, and Brahms constitutes the backbone of the clarinet repertoire.

In 1870 Heinrich Baermann's son Carl, also a clarinetist, together with his grandson, Carl, a noted pianist with the intention to recreate the works as Heinrich played them published a revised edition of all of Weber's works for clarinet. While Carl Baermann's revision has formed the basis of most subsequent editions and has had a major influence on the performance tradition of these works, it has recently, often with very good reason, come under serious criticism for capriciously distorting Weber's original text.

While I have been one of those critics, I do not believe that Baermann's revisions are completely worthless. While the standard criticism suggests that Carl who grew up in a later Romantic age (he played in the premiere of Wagner's "Tristan and Isolde") applied the aesthetic of that age to Weber's music of an earlier time, I would beg to differ that he was, on the contrary, trying to preserve, perhaps in a clumsy way, the performance tradition of an earlier time. In rewriting rhythms, he was trying to recapture the kind of rubato which Weber would have expected - elongating important notes, bringing out appoggiaturas, by adding ornaments, he was trying restore what earlier would have been natural additions to the music. Baermann's own notation, however, led to many misinterpretations.

In this edition, I have chosen to present Weber's original text together with my own suggestions and in notes to indicate what from Baermann's edition I find interesting and useful. Also for contrast, I have presented examples from Cyrille Rose's edition of 1879 which formed the basis of the French Weber performance tradition and which held much more closely to Weber's original. By presenting Weber's wonderful Concertino in this way, I hope to inspire those learning the piece to develop their own personal, yet informed interpretation. I am sure that this would be what Weber would have desired.

CONCERTINO in E♭ MAJOR, Op. 26
for Clarinet in B♭ and Piano

Edited by Charles Neidich
Piano Part Revised by Charles Neidich

CARL MARIA von WEBER
(1786–1826)

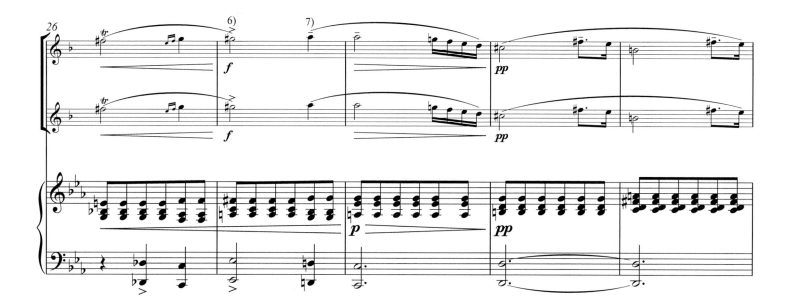

Thema[10)]
Andante

Thema
Andante

Poco più vivo

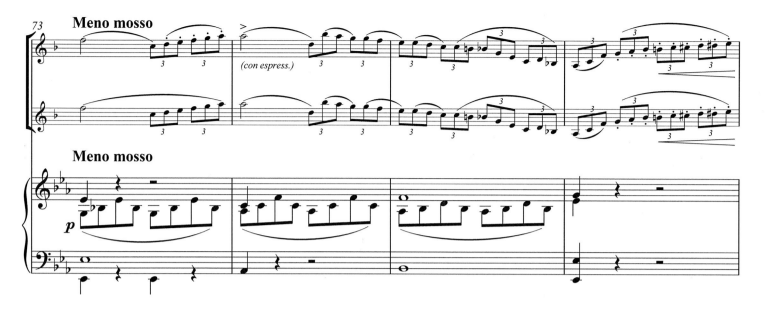

poco rallentando   a tempo

poco rallentando   a tempo

Carl Maria von WEBER

CONCERTINO FOR CLARINET

Edited by Charles Neidich

Clarinet in Bb

Weber Concertino, Introduction

It was a wonderful accident of fate which brought the young composer Carl Maria von Weber together in 1811 with the great clarinet virtuoso Heinrich Baermann. Weber met Baermann in the town of Darmstadt sometime early in 1811 and having been engaged for a concert in Munich, Baermann's hometown, he asked if Baermann would like to collaborate. Baermann, at that time the more famous of the two, agreed on condition that Weber compose a work for him to play. Weber complied with the Concertino which he finished in three days on April 3rd. Baermann performed the work on April 5 and just two days after, on April 7th the King of Bavaria, who was very impressed both with the work itself and with Baermann's virtuosic rendition, commissioned Weber to write 2 concertos. These Weber soon competed and Baermann premiered both in the same year, the first on June 13 and the second on November 25. Weber went on to write two more works for Baermann, the Variations, op. 33 and the Quintet op. 48. The Gran Duo Concertante, composed most likely for Baermann's colleague and rival, Johann Hermstedt completed Weber's oeuvre for clarinet, a body of work which along with that of Mozart, Spohr, and Brahms constitutes the backbone of the clarinet repertoire.

In 1870 Heinrich Baermann's son Carl, also a clarinetist, together with his grandson, Carl, a noted pianist with the intention to recreate the works as Heinrich played them published a revised edition of all of Weber's works for clarinet. While Carl Baermann's revision has formed the basis of most subsequent editions and has had a major influence on the performance tradition of these works, it has recently, often with very good reason, come under serious criticism for capriciously distorting Weber's original text.

While I have been one of those critics, I do not believe that Baermann's revisions are completely worthless. While the standard criticism suggests that Carl who grew up in a later Romantic age (he played in the premiere of Wagner's "Tristan and Isolde") applied the aesthetic of that age to Weber's music of an earlier time, I would beg to differ that he was, on the contrary, trying to preserve, perhaps in a clumsy way, the performance tradition of an earlier time. In rewriting rhythms, he was trying to recapture the kind of rubato which Weber would have expected - elongating important notes, bringing out appoggiaturas, by adding ornaments, he was trying restore what earlier would have been natural additions to the music. Baermann's own notation, however, led to many misinterpretations.

In this edition, I have chosen to present Weber's original text together with my own suggestions and in notes to indicate what from Baermann's edition I find interesting and useful. Also for contrast, I have presented examples from Cyrille Rose's edition of 1879 which formed the basis of the French Weber performance tradition and which held much more closely to Weber's original. By presenting Weber's wonderful Concertino in this way, I hope to inspire those learning the piece to develop their own personal, yet informed interpretation. I am sure that this would be what Weber would have desired.

Clarinet in B♭   # CONCERTINO in E♭ MAJOR, Op. 26
for Clarinet in B♭ and Piano

3

Edited by Charles Neidich

CARL MARIA von WEBER
(1786–1826)

Four Cadenzas

(m. 146)

CHARLES NEIDICH

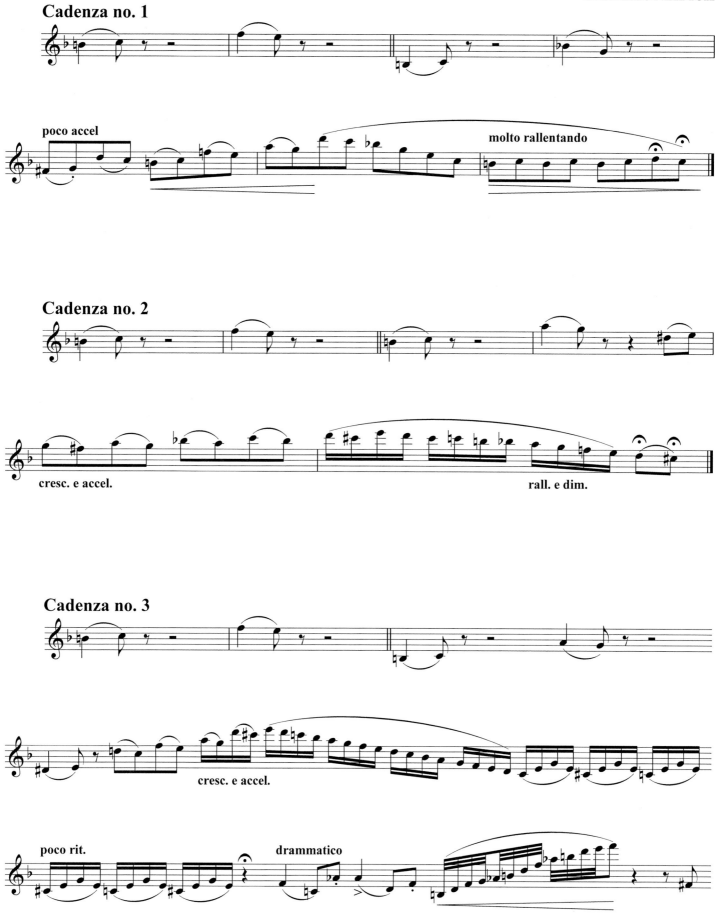

poco adagio

a piacere   rallentando

Cadenza no. 4

p cresc. e molto accelerando

ritardando molto e dim.

Notes

1) m. 2

Note about the accent as used by Weber.

Weber did not use the tenuto sign (−), but used the accent (>) most often to indicate tenuto, importance of the note, or an expressive leaning on the note. I have left his markings intact, but when I have added an indication of expressive leaning (appoggiatura), I have used the tenuto to distinguish from what Weber wrote.

2) m. 3

A note about Weber's use of the "wedge."

He used it, as previous composers such as Mozart and contemporaries such as Beethoven did, to indicate important notes which should be emphasized. These are not necessarily short notes and are often long and heavy. Carl Baermann did not include them in his edition, because he felt they were old fashioned. I believe, on the contrary, that once one understands their meaning, they become very clear indicators of how to phrase, and have chosen to keep them without alteration.

3) m. 13

The F appoggiatura should be long, at least an eighth note.

4) m. 18

This notation was considered "old fashioned" by Carl Baermann, but I much prefer it to what Baermann decided to use. For Weber, as for composers in the eighteenth century and early nineteenth century in general, the slur with dots meant a long expressive portato, often played with rubato. It has also been called a "singing" or "articulated" legato. Weber used one slur under the entire passage instead of one from the G to A and another beginning on the F (as Cyrille Rose revised the marking) because that would have indicated that he wanted a shortened A and a comma between the two parts of the passage rather than one gesture with added expression in the second half.

5) m. 24

Ornaments such as turns should be played in rhythm. It is important to know on what fraction of which beat one is putting the ornament.

6) m. 27. Weber did not place a trill over the G♯ in m. 27, but rather indicated with the accent (tenuto, see Note 1) that that is the end of that phrase. This you can see clearly in the accompaniment bass part. In the initial measure Weber writes a trill over the clarinet F♯ and a rest on the first beat in the bass. The next measure F♯ has an accent and no trill and the E♭ in the bass Weber places on the first beat with an accent, not on the second beat as would be expected had Weber wanted a trill on G♯ in the clarinet.

7) m. 27. Weber begins the new phrase not on the downbeat of the next measure, but on the third beat G in m. 27. Having the first phrase end on the G♯ and the next phrase begin on the upbeat G creates a much more beautiful and sophisticated phrase than Baermann's reinterpretation.

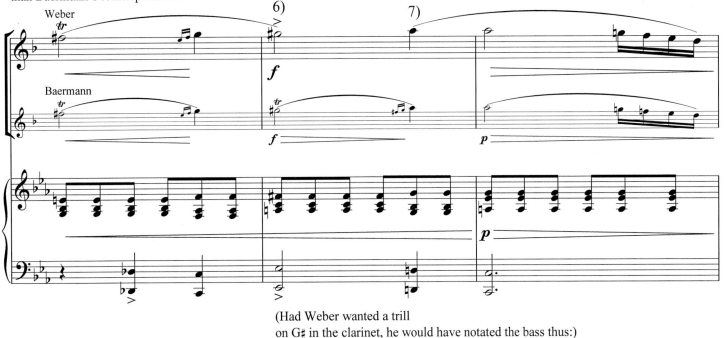

(Had Weber wanted a trill
on G♯ in the clarinet, he would have notated the bass thus:)

8) m. 31

Baermann added a turn to the D before the last F. He also put a dot on the F. I do not include this, because for my taste it makes the passage awkwardly cluttered. It is, however, an acceptable ornament. At the time Weber wrote the Concertino, it was very normal for performers to ornament the pieces they were playing, and one's creativity and tastefullnes in ornamenting pieces was a sign of musical prowess and sophistication. Heinrich Baermann definitely would have ornamented both this piece and all the others Weber wrote for him.

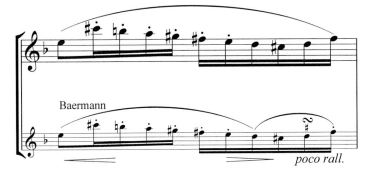

9) m. 35

The "sigh motif with which Weber ended the introduction two preliminary times in mm. 32 and 33 and finally in m. 35 is the major motif of the Concertino. It reappears as the theme and after that comes back in various guises. It should always be played in a way which makes it clear. Here are a few examples. An interesting project would be to find all the times Weber uses this motif.

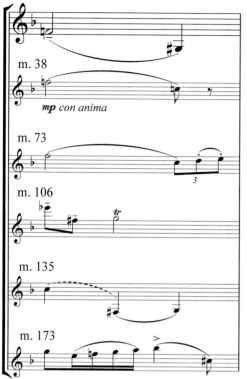

10) m. 38. Baermann added several expression marks to Weber's score to indicate the different characters of the variations and consequently to indicate their different tempi. I believe they are well thought out and have decided to include them in the score in parentheses and italics. They are the following: m. 38 *Thema*, m. 54 *Poco più vivo*, m. 73 *Meno mosso*, m. 74 *con espress.*, m. 96 *Poco più vivo*, m. 125 *Lento*, m. 163 *risoluto*, m. 165 *dolce*, m. 185 *con passione*, m. 211 *con fuoco*.

While Weber did not indicate differences in tempo for individual variations, it is hard to believe he would not have assumed that performers would choose tempi according to the characters of the different variations. If we look at what can be called standard classical variations form, we find the following form: theme; first variation very closely connected to the theme and, therefore, basically the same tempo; second variation, often more virtuosic and, therefore, faster; third variation, very calm character, often with a tempo marking of Adagio; final variation, Allegro, as befits a finale. Weber basically followed this form with an interesting and creative difference. Between the theme and the first variation, he included a virtuosic interlude. After that, the variations follow in classical order: first, very closely related to the theme; second, virtuosic; third, calm and somber; finale, quick and exciting, befitting a finale. Weber, of course, would have assumed that Heinrich Baermann, or whoever else would perform the work, would understand the basic form, and, therefore, would not have felt the pressing need to provide different tempo markings. Just consider how absurd the third variation beginning at m. 125 would sound at the tempo of the previous variation— it needs the repose of a slower tempo—or how boring the interlude after the theme would sound at the same tempo as the theme, or how silly the theme would sound at the fast tempo of the interlude.

11) m. 69

12) m. 82

Suggested execution

13) m. 96. Weber, as you can see, wrote almost no articulations for this variation. The clarinet part contains my suggestions. Below, for the sake of information are those of Carl Baermann and also those of Cyrille Rose as published around 1879. It is interesting to note that Rose's editions generally followed Weber's original more closely than Baermann's.

Carl Bärmann edition, Robert Lienau, Berlin ca. 1870

Cyrille Rose edition, Evette & Schaeffer ca. 1879?

In m. 102, the dotted high D and the 32nd note E after as written by Baermann deserves explanation. In trying to reproduce what he considered to be correct performance practice, he wanted to show that the final E was part of the next measure's arpeggio. He also wanted to show that the arpeggio in m. 102 should be played with a certain amount of bravura and rubato. Thus, he lengthened the high D and rewrote the E as a 32nd note with a staccato dot on top. He did not, however, expect that anyone would literally play the dotted 16th and 32nd. I tried to notate a similar separation in a more subtle way with a comma after the D and a dot over the E. Baermann, one should realize, did not have the comma (or the tenuto dash) in his repertoire of markings.

14) mm. 102, 110. Two suggested possible articulations.

15) m. 110. I suggest, as in the Cyrille Rose edition, going up to the high F. If not, play as in m. 102.

16) m. 146. Weber expected the performer to play a cadenza here. Soloists would most often improvise cadenzas (just as they would improvise ornaments), but would also on occasion write them down. Baermann did write a cadenza of which, personally, I am not enamored. I have provided four possible cadenzas of my own of varying lengths (pp. 8 and 9) and difficulty which may be used directly or which may form the basis of one's own attempts at cadenza writing and performing.

17) m. 176

I can imagine several possible articulations for this passage and the equivalent one in m. 178, so I prefer to leave it up to the performer's choice, just as Weber did.

18) m. 177

Awkwardness in this passage comes from the first half of the measure having only six notes and the second half thirteen notes. To make it more fluid, I would even it out so the first half has nine and the second half ten.

19) m. 211

While Baermann's revision is generally played (sometimes with Rose's variation in m. 219), Weber's original is both more virtuosic and more imaginative with his emphasis on the last eighth notes of the measures, with his playful false cadence on the downbeat of m. 215, and especially with his perky rhythm in m. 219. I strongly suggest playing Weber's original version.

Cyrille Rose

20) m. 223

This passage and the following ones in mm. 225 and 227 can be smoothed out as below:

Suggested execution

21) m. 229

Below are Baermann's and Rose's articulations. In my opinion, many different articulations (including all tongued) are possible, so I prefer to leave the choice, as Weber did, to the performer.

Baermann

Rose

22) m. 235

Baermann added a run up to the high E trill. I kept the original, only adding a *nachschlag*, but the run, of course, would be a perfectly acceptable ornament.

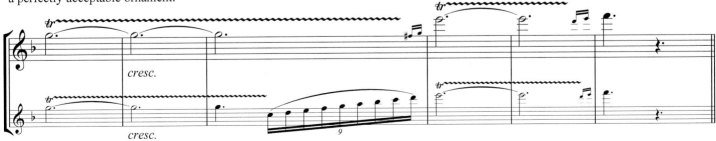

cresc.

cresc.

Charles Neidich
21st Century Series for Clarinet

Charles Neidich, hailed by the New Yorker as "a master of his instrument and beyond a clarinetist", has been described as one of the most mesmerizing musicians performing today. Mr. Neidich is on the faculties of the Juilliard School, Queens College of the City University of New York, the Manhattan School, and the Mannes College of Music, and has held visiting positions at the Sibelius Academy in Finland, the Yale School of Music, and Michigan State University. He regularly appears as soloist and as collaborator in programs with major orchestras and chamber ensembles across Europe, Asia, and the United States. Neidich is in demand for master classes throughout the world and known for innovative lecture concerts he has devised. Known both as a leading exponent of period instrument performance practice and as an ardent advocate of new music, Charles Neidich's recordings are available on the Sony Classical, Sony Vivarte, Deutsche Grammophon, Musicmasters, Hyperion, and Bridge labels.

WEBER CONCERTINO FOR CLARINET
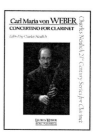
Written for virtuoso clarinetist Heinrich Baermann, Concertino would become the first work of an impressive oeuvre for clarinet, one which along with that of Mozart, Spohr, and Brahms constitutes the backbone of the repertoire. Internationally-recognized clarinetist Charles Neidich unites for the first time Weber's original text with the edition published by Baermann's son, which had formed the basis of most subsequent editions. Also presented are examples from Cyrille Rose's 1879 edition which was the foundation of the French tradition and which held much more closely to Weber's original. This new critical edition inspires those learning the piece to develop their own personal, yet informed interpretation of Weber's premiere clarinet masterpiece. HL00111948...$10.95

ROSSINI INTRODUCTION, THEME AND VARIATIONS FOR CLARINET
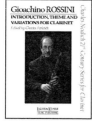
The work is based on two of Rossini's most moving dramatic arias and remains one of the most popular virtuosic works for clarinet to this day. This critical edition by celebrated clarinetist Charles Neidich takes a fresh approach to this work, blending the 19th Century bel canto traditions with a master's perspective on modern clarinet technique. Detailed annotations and historical background equip the clarinetist with an in-depth musical and technical facility to authentically convey the characteristic elegance and drama of Rossini's style. HL00111949 ....$10.95

CAVALLINI 30 CAPRICES FOR CLARINET WITH 2 CD'S

Cavallini was called the 'Paganini of the Clarinet' and was a respected friend and colleague of the most important Italian composers of his day. His 30 Caprices were written to be not merely technical exercises, but studies in style and phrasing. In addition to correcting mistakes and modernizing notation, the noteworthy feature of this edition is clarinetist Charles Neidich's superb recording which is the only complete recording of this classic work. HL00042367 ....$22.95

JEANJEAN 18 ADVANCED ETUDES FOR CLARINET WITH 2 CD'S

Jeanjean, a great virtuoso and prolific writer for the clarinet, attempted in his 18 etudes to write pieces which in addition to being very beneficial to one's technique, would be serious works of music fit for the concert stage. Editor Charles Neidich, hailed by the New Yorker as "a master of his instrument and beyond a clarinetist", brings Jeanjean's Etudes into fresh perspective in this new performance edition. Along with modern, corrected notation and fingerings, the only complete recording is included to demonstrate a characteristic interpretation of the Etudes and to inspire students to explore creative possibilities informed by tradition in their own performances. HL00042385 ....$20.95

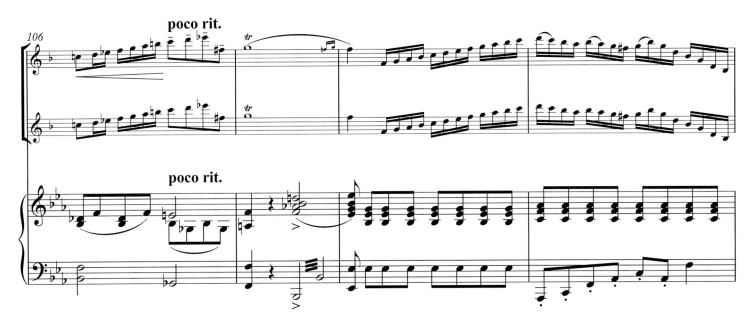

(timpani)

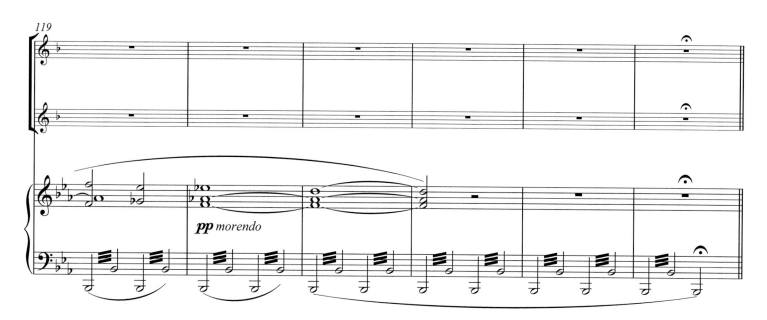

(timpani)

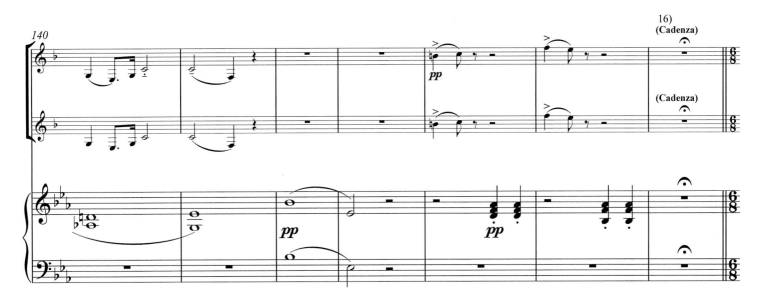

14

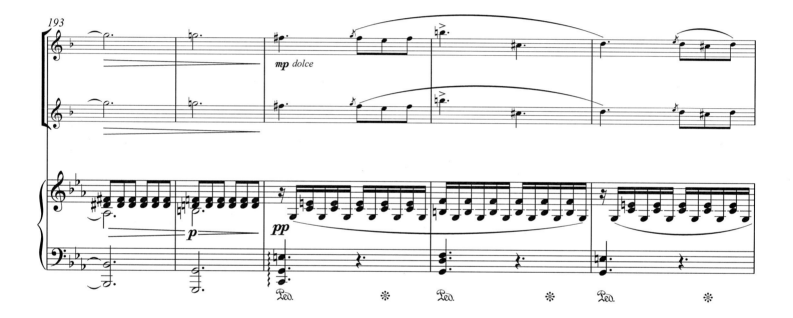

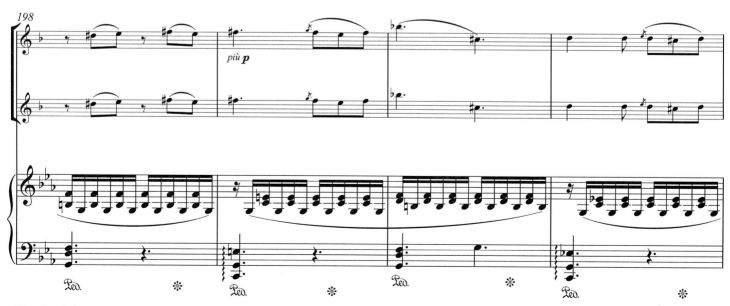

Charles Neidich

21st Century Series for Clarinet

Charles Neidich, hailed by the New Yorker as "a master of his instrument and beyond a clarinetist", has been described as one of the most mesmerizing musicians performing today. Mr. Neidich is on the faculties of the Juilliard School, Queens College of the City University of New York, the Manhattan School, and the Mannes College of Music, and has held visiting positions at the Sibelius Academy in Finland, the Yale School of Music, and Michigan State University. He regularly appears as soloist and as collaborator in programs with major orchestras and chamber ensembles across Europe, Asia, and the United States. Neidich is in demand for master classes throughout the world and known for innovative lecture concerts he has devised. Known both as a leading exponent of period instrument performance practice and as an ardent advocate of new music, Charles Neidich's recordings are available on the Sony Classical, Sony Vivarte, Deutsche Grammophon, Musicmasters, Hyperion, and Bridge labels.

WEBER CONCERTINO FOR CLARINET

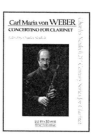

Written for virtuoso clarinetist Heinrich Baermann, Concertino would become the first work of an impressive oeuvre for clarinet, one which along with that of Mozart, Spohr, and Brahms constitutes the backbone of the repertoire. Internationally-recognized clarinetist Charles Neidich unites for the first time Weber's original text with the edition published by Baermann's son, which had formed the basis of most subsequent editions. Also presented are examples from Cyrille Rose's 1879 edition which was the foundation of the French tradition and which held much more closely to Weber's original. This new critical edition inspires those learning the piece to develop their own personal, yet informed interpretation of Weber's premiere clarinet masterpiece. HL00111948..$10.95

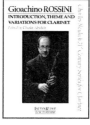

ROSSINI INTRODUCTION, THEME AND VARIATIONS FOR CLARINET

The work is based on two of Rossini's most moving dramatic arias and remains one of the most popular virtuosic works for clarinet to this day. This critical edition by celebrated clarinetist Charles Neidich takes a fresh approach to this work, blending the 19th Century bel canto traditions with a master's perspective on modern clarinet technique. Detailed annotations and historical background equip the clarinetist with an in-depth musical and technical facility to authentically convey the characteristic elegance and drama of Rossini's style. HL00111949 ....$10.95

CAVALLINI 30 CAPRICES FOR CLARINET WITH 2 CD'S

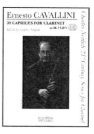

Cavallini was called the 'Paganini of the Clarinet' and was a respected friend and colleague of the most important Italian composers of his day. His 30 Caprices were written to be not merely technical exercises, but studies in style and phrasing. In addition to correcting mistakes and modernizing notation, the noteworthy feature of this edition is clarinetist Charles Neidich's superb recording which is the only complete recording of this classic work. HL00042367 ....$22.95

JEANJEAN 18 ADVANCED ETUDES FOR CLARINET WITH 2 CD'S

Jeanjean, a great virtuoso and prolific writer for the clarinet, attempted in his 18 etudes to write pieces which in addition to being very beneficial to one's technique, would be serious works of music fit for the concert stage. Editor Charles Neidich, hailed by the New Yorker as "a master of his instrument and beyond a clarinetist", brings Jeanjean's Etudes into fresh perspective in this new performance edition. Along with modern, corrected notation and fingerings, the only complete recording is included to demonstrate a characteristic interpretation of the Etudes and to inspire students to explore creative possibilities informed by tradition in their own performances. HL00042385 ....$20.95

Products and Ordering
www.halleonard.com

Questions or comments?
info@laurenkeisermusic.com